A CHARLIE BROWN CHRISTMAS
FOR SOLO JAZZ GUITAR

© PEANUTS Worldwide LLC

Arranged by Pete Billmann

ISBN 978-1-70516-825-7

For all works contained herein:
Unauthorized copying, arranging, adapting, recording, internet posting, public performance,
or other distribution of the music in this publication is an infringement of copyright.
Infringers are liable under the law.

© 2022 PEANUTS Worldwide LLC
www.snoopy.com

Visit Hal Leonard Online at
www.halleonard.com

World headquarters, contact:
Hal Leonard
7777 West Bluemound Road
Milwaukee, WI 53213
Email: info@halleonard.com

In Europe, contact:
Hal Leonard Europe Limited
1 Red Place
London, W1K 6PL
Email: info@halleonardeurope.com

In Australia, contact:
Hal Leonard Australia Pty. Ltd.
4 Lentara Court
Cheltenham, Victoria, 3192 Australia
Email: info@halleonard.com.au

© PEANUTS Worldwide LLC

© PEANUTS Worldwide LLC

O Tannenbaum

Traditional
Arranged by Vince Guaraldi

Copyright © 1966 LEE MENDELSON FILM PRODUCTIONS, INC.
Copyright Renewed
This arrangement Copyright © 2022 LEE MENDELSON FILM PRODUCTIONS, INC.
International Copyright Secured   All Rights Reserved

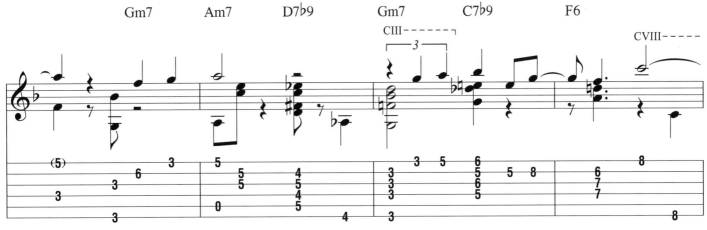

To Coda ⊕

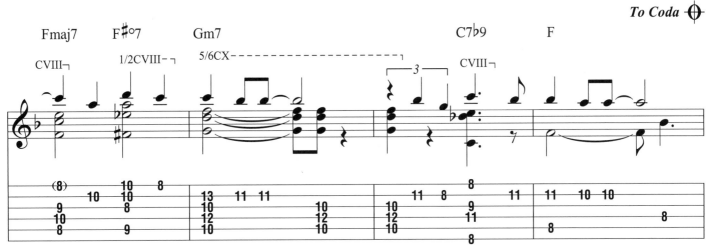

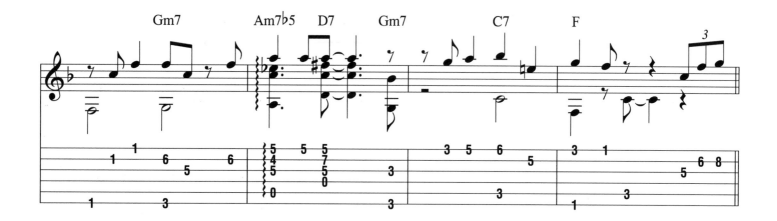

C

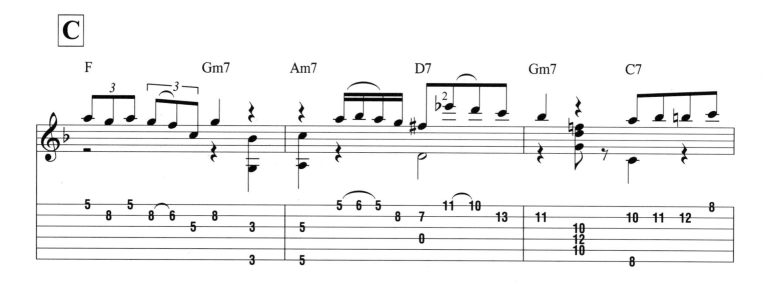

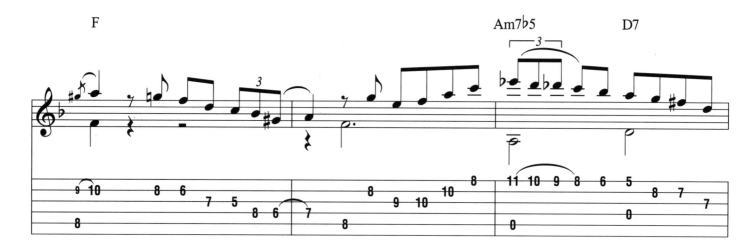

D.S. al Coda

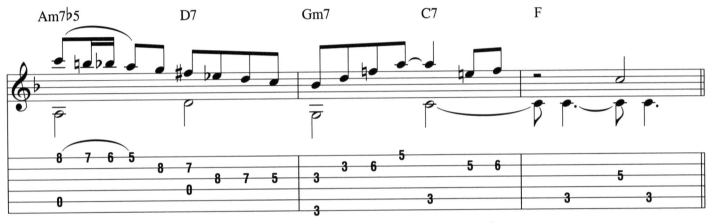

⊕ **Coda**

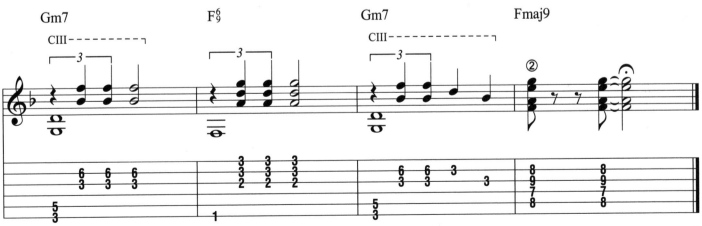

What Child Is This

Traditional
Arranged by Vince Guaraldi

A

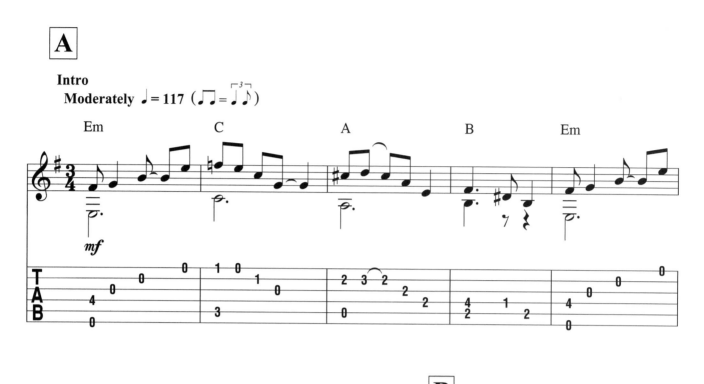

B

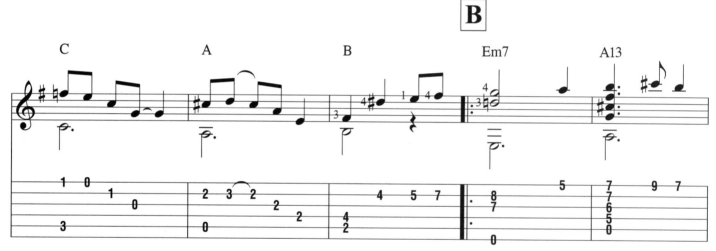

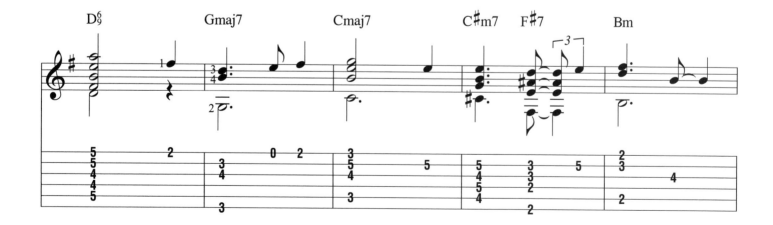

Copyright © 1966 LEE MENDELSON FILM PRODUCTIONS, INC.
Copyright Renewed
This arrangement Copyright © 2022 LEE MENDELSON FILM PRODUCTIONS, INC.
International Copyright Secured   All Rights Reserved

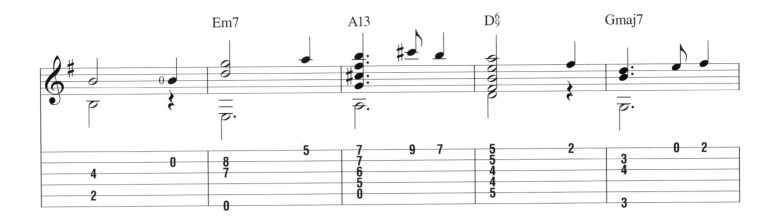

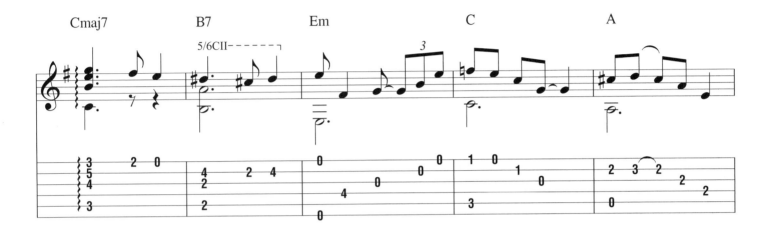

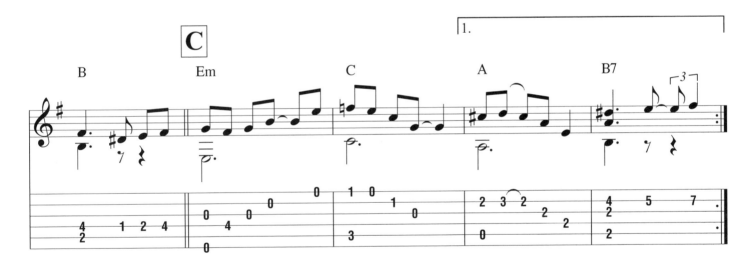

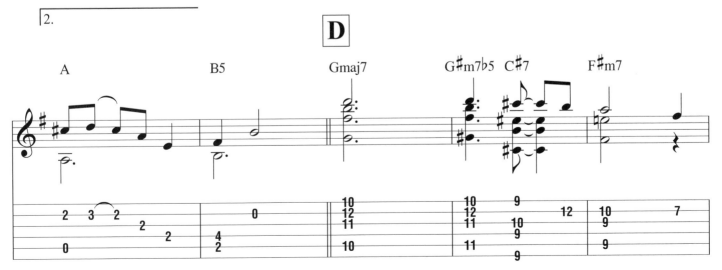

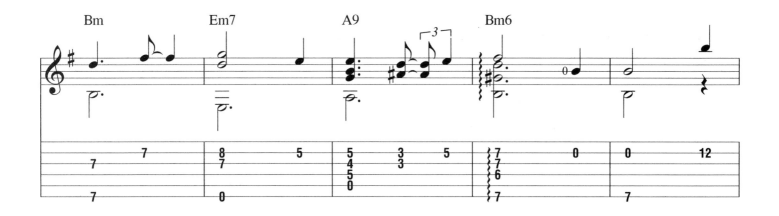

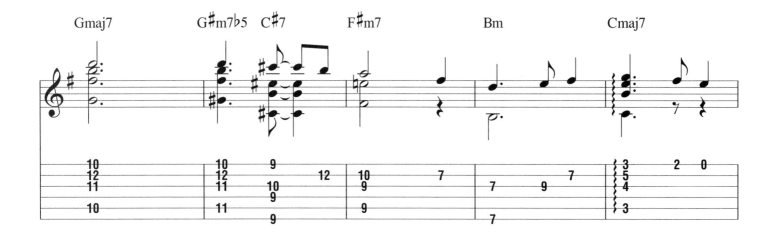

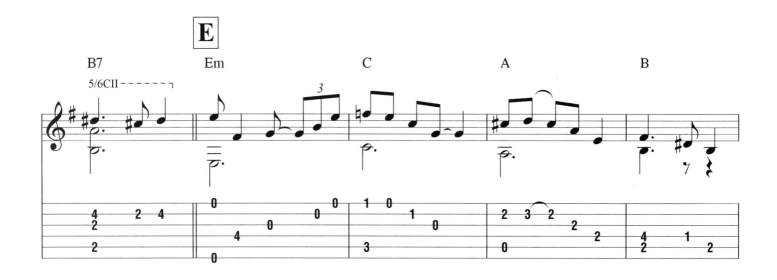

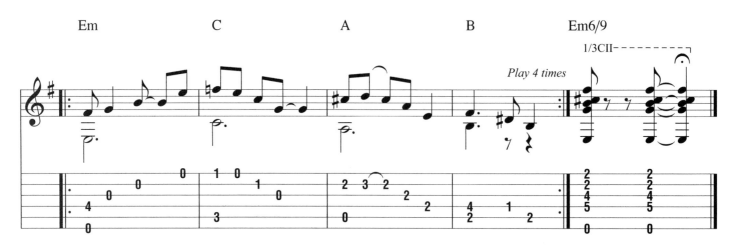

My Little Drum

By Vince Guaraldi

*Chord symbols reflect implied harmony.

Copyright © 1966 LEE MENDELSON FILM PRODUCTIONS, INC.
Copyright Renewed
This arrangement Copyright © 2022 LEE MENDELSON FILM PRODUCTIONS, INC.
International Copyright Secured   All Rights Reserved

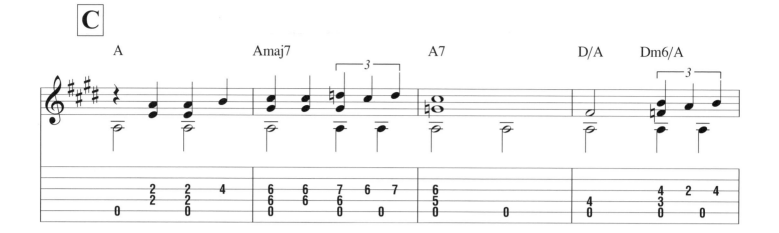

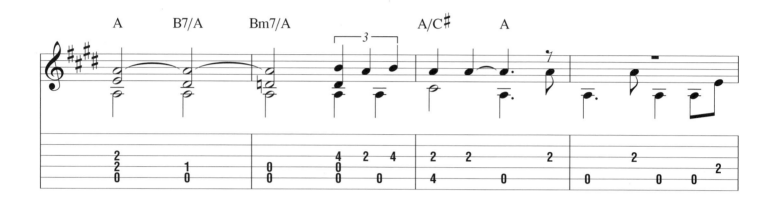

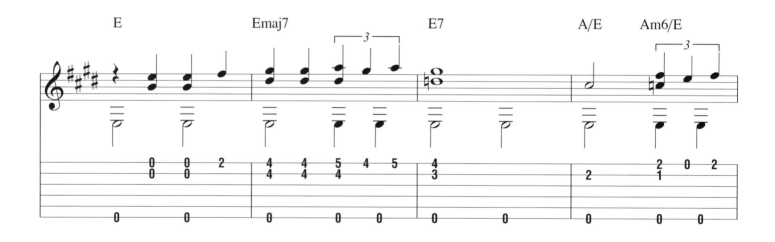

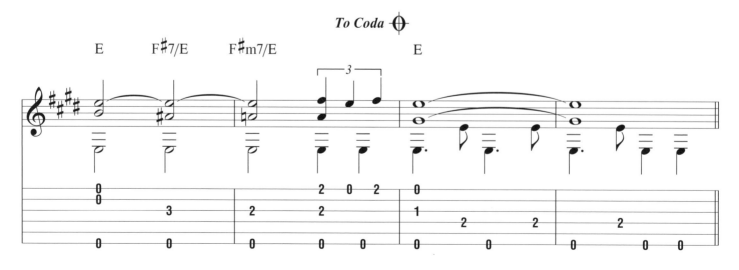

D

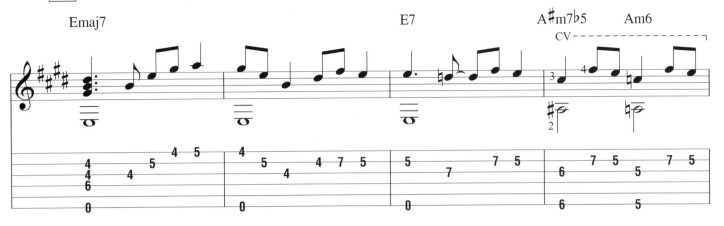

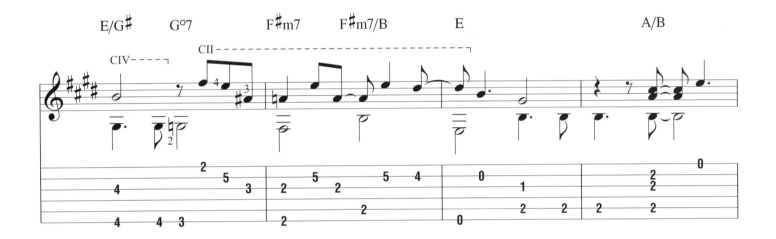

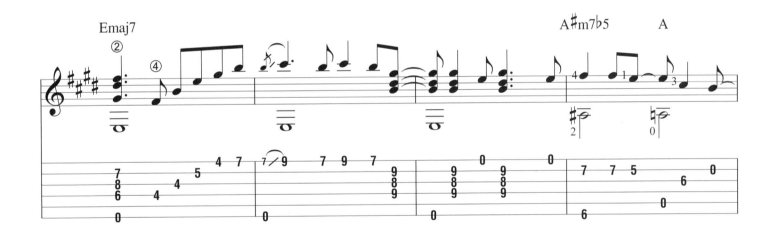

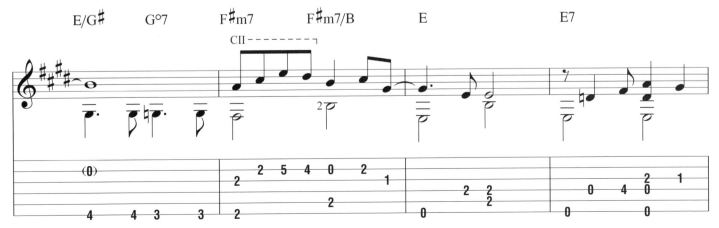

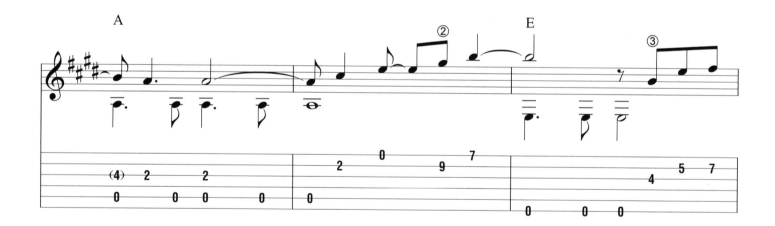

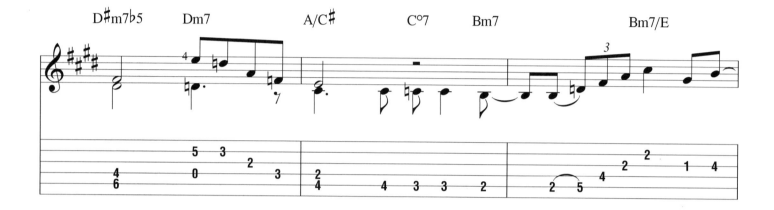

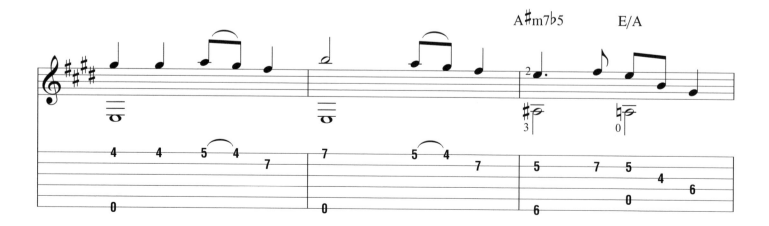

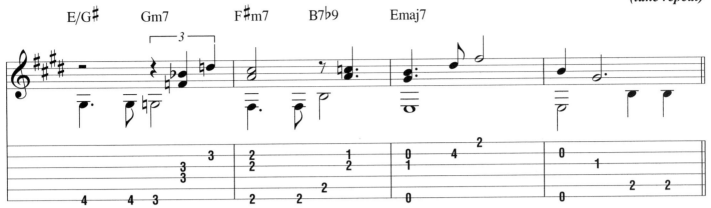

⊕ **Coda**

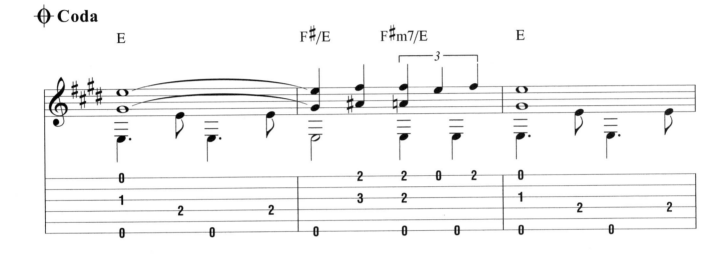

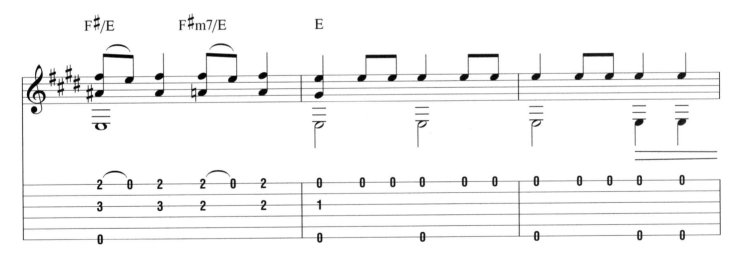

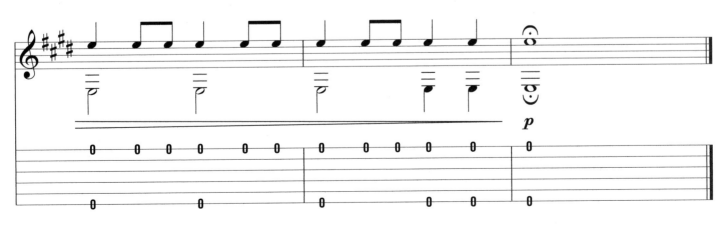

Linus and Lucy

By Vince Guaraldi

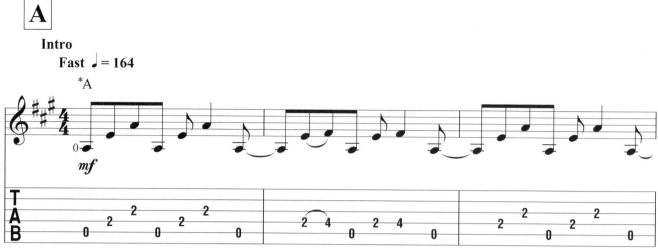

*Chord symbols reflect implied harmony.

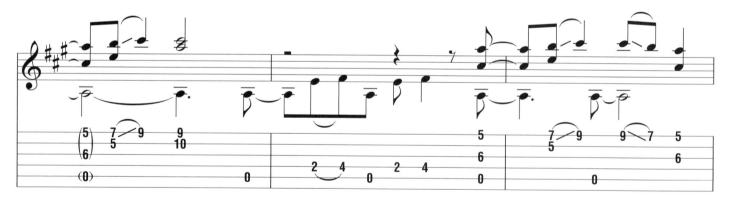

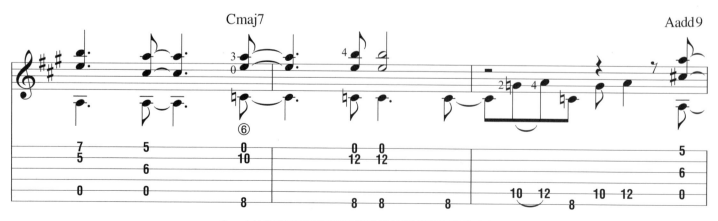

Copyright © 1965 LEE MENDELSON FILM PRODUCTIONS, INC.
Copyright Renewed
This arrangement Copyright © 2022 LEE MENDELSON FILM PRODUCTIONS, INC.
International Copyright Secured   All Rights Reserved

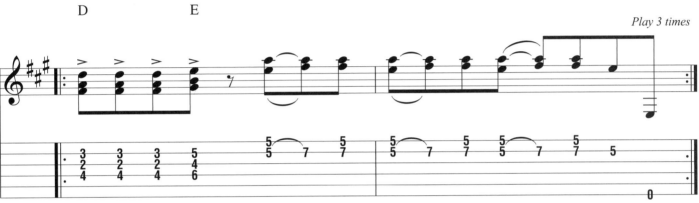

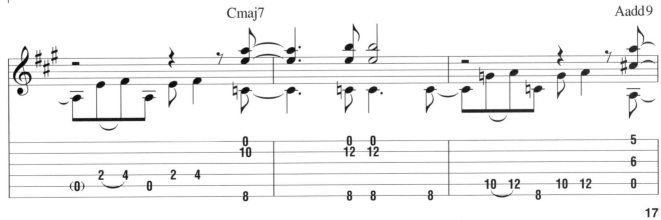

D

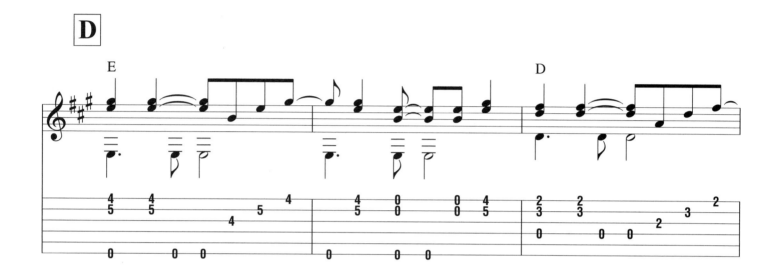

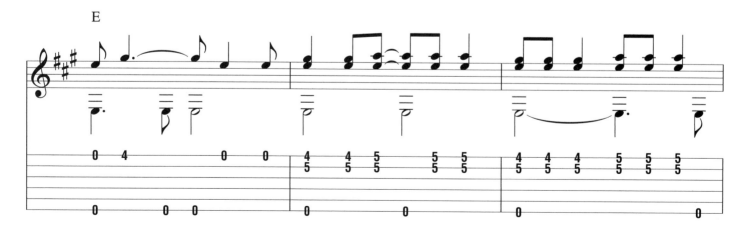

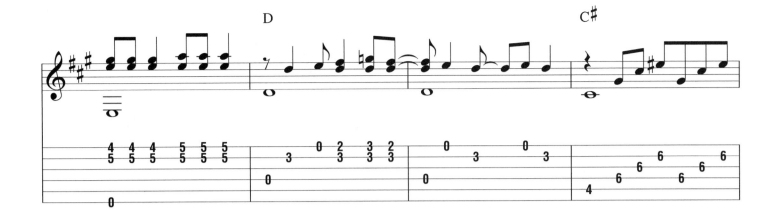

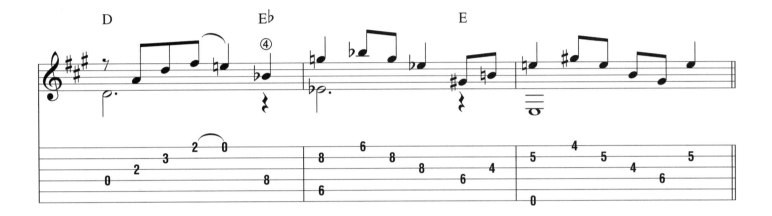

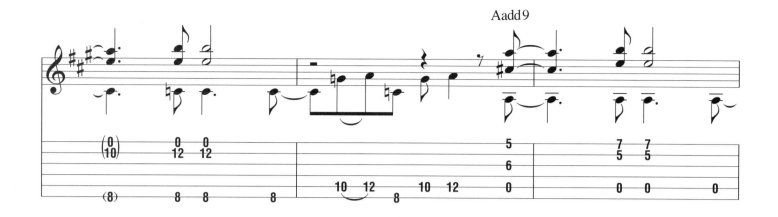

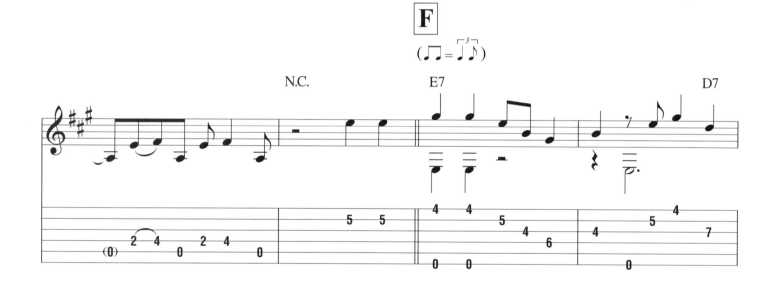

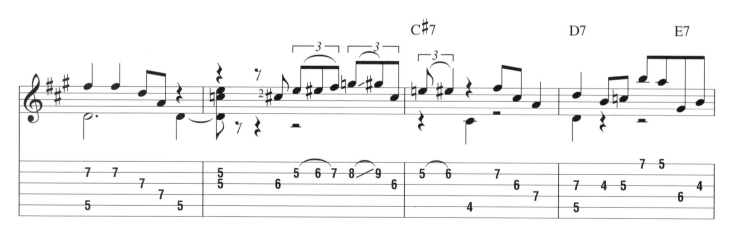

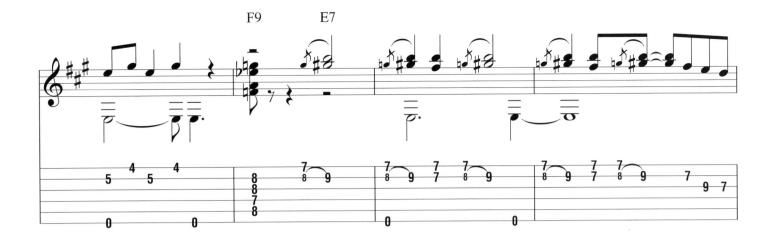

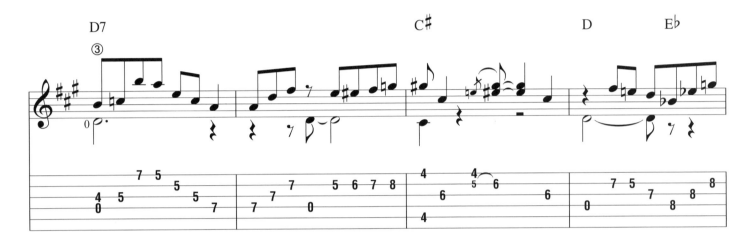

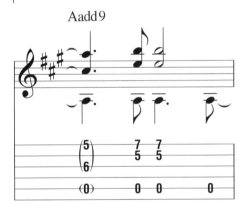

D.S.S. al Coda 2

Coda 2

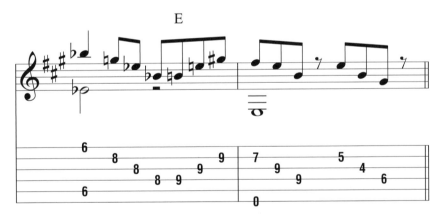

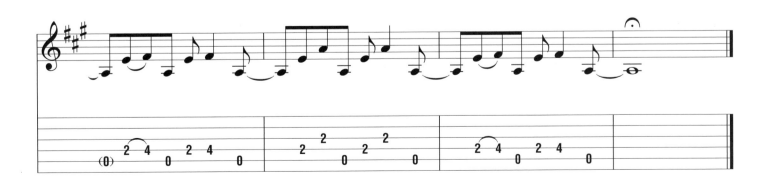

Christmas Time Is Here

Words by Lee Mendelson
Music by Vince Guaraldi

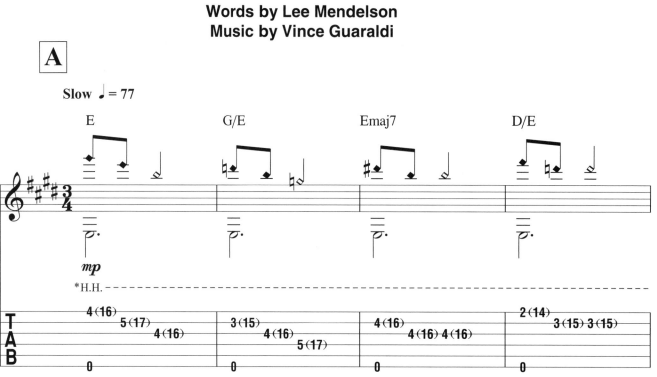

*Harp harmonics produced by lightly touching strings 12 frets above fretted notes while picking strings.

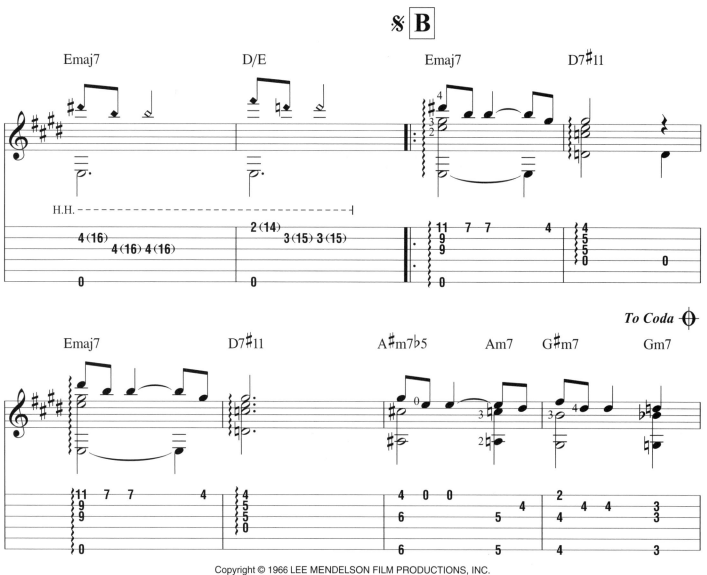

Copyright © 1966 LEE MENDELSON FILM PRODUCTIONS, INC.
Copyright Renewed
This arrangement Copyright © 2022 LEE MENDELSON FILM PRODUCTIONS, INC.
International Copyright Secured   All Rights Reserved

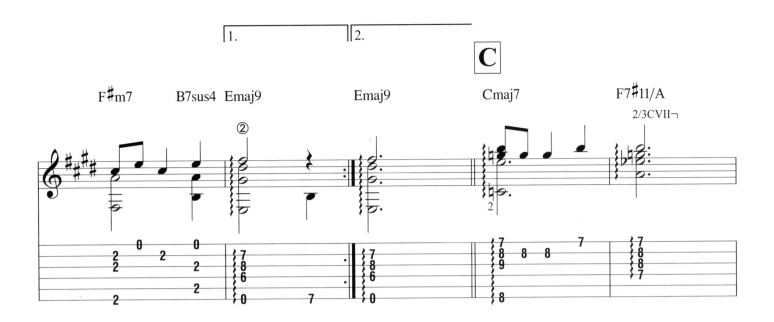

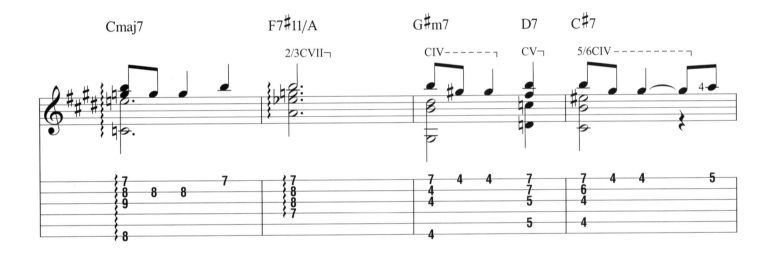

1st time, D.S. (take 2nd ending)
2nd time, D.S. al Coda

Coda

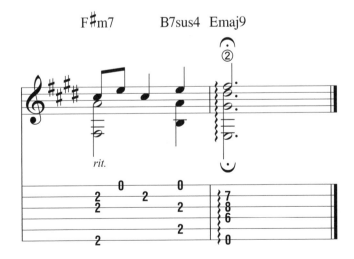

Skating

By Vince Guaraldi

A

Intro
Fast ♩ = 194

℠ B

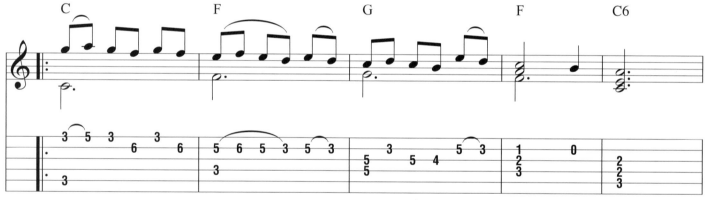

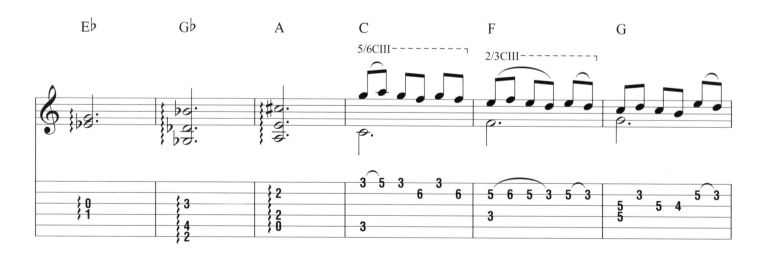

Copyright © 1966 LEE MENDELSON FILM PRODUCTIONS, INC.
Copyright Renewed
This arrangement Copyright © 2022 LEE MENDELSON FILM PRODUCTIONS, INC.
International Copyright Secured   All Rights Reserved

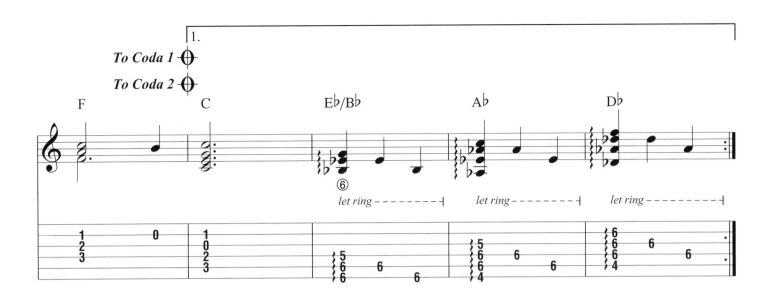

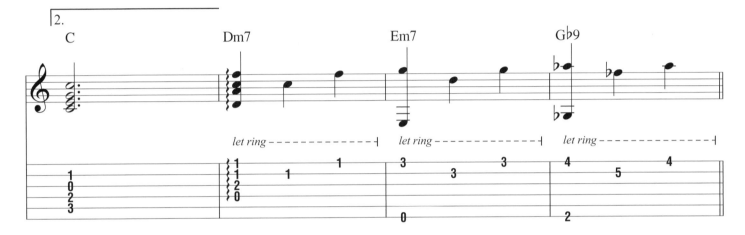

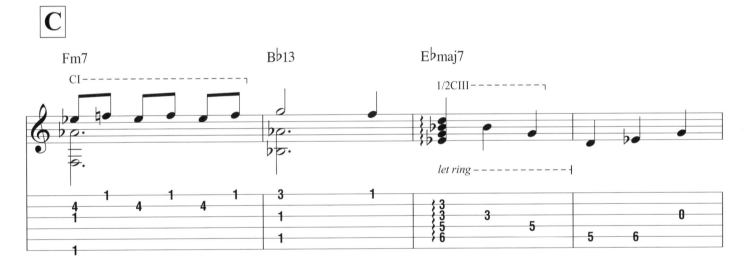

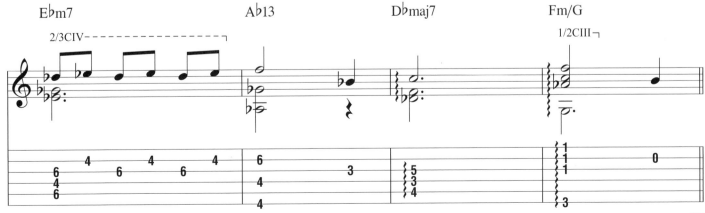

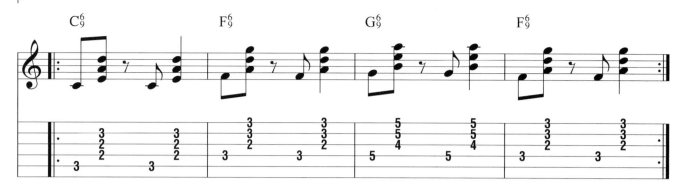

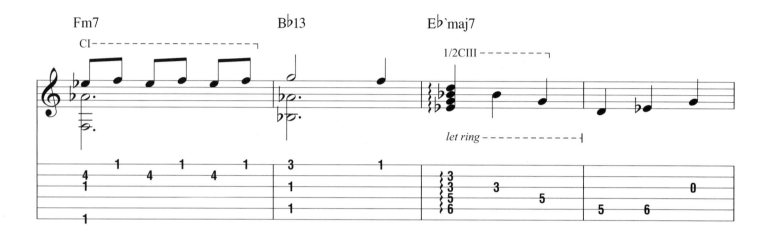

D.S. al Coda 2

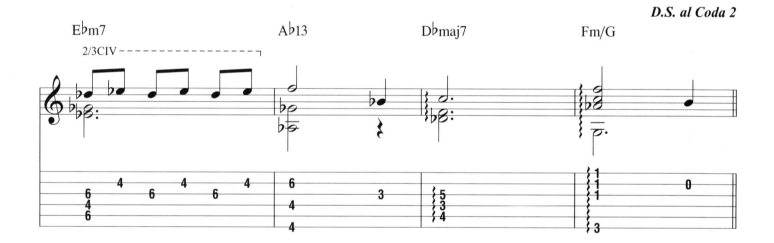

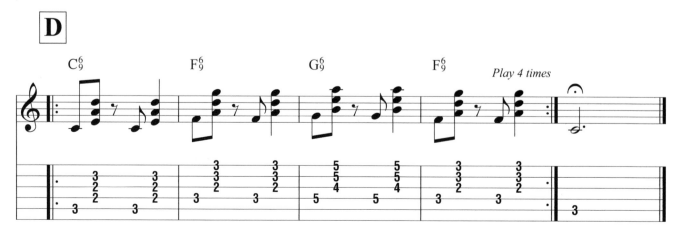

Hark, the Herald Angels Sing

Traditional
Arranged by Vince Guaraldi

Copyright © 1965 LEE MENDELSON FILM PRODUCTIONS, INC.
Copyright Renewed
This arrangement Copyright © 2022 LEE MENDELSON FILM PRODUCTIONS, INC.
International Copyright Secured   All Rights Reserved

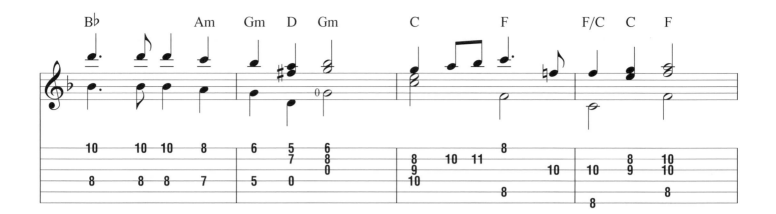

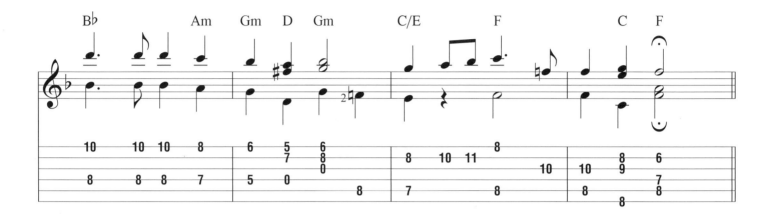

B

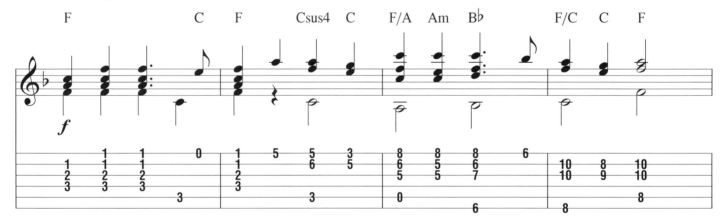

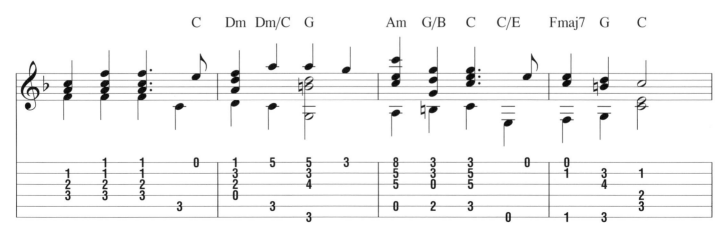

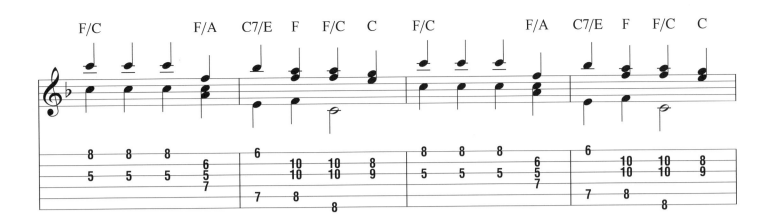

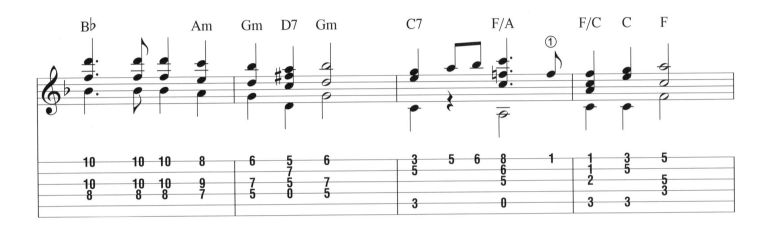

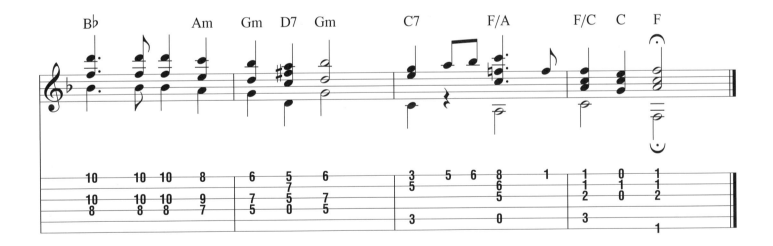

Christmas Is Coming

By Vince Guaraldi

Copyright © 1966 LEE MENDELSON FILM PRODUCTIONS, INC.
Copyright Renewed
This arrangement Copyright © 2022 LEE MENDELSON FILM PRODUCTIONS, INC.
International Copyright Secured   All Rights Reserved

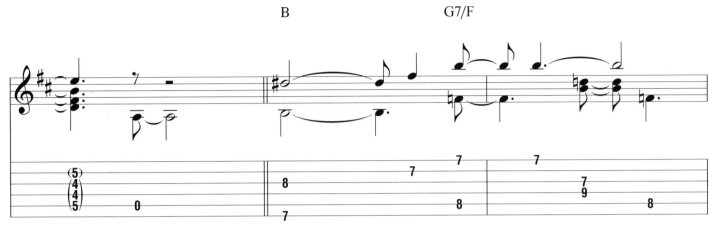

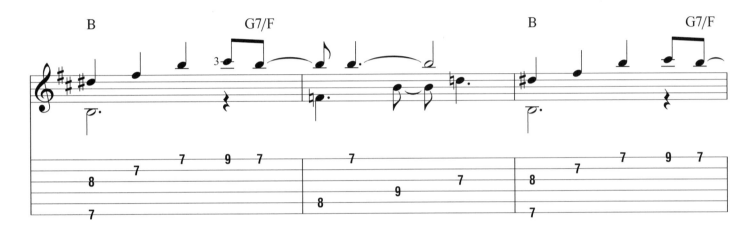

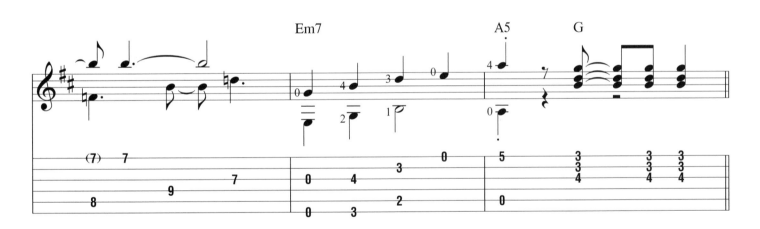

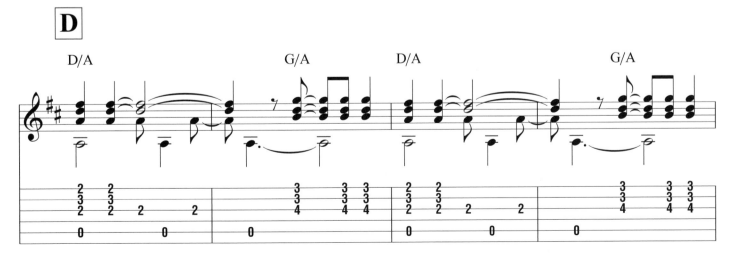

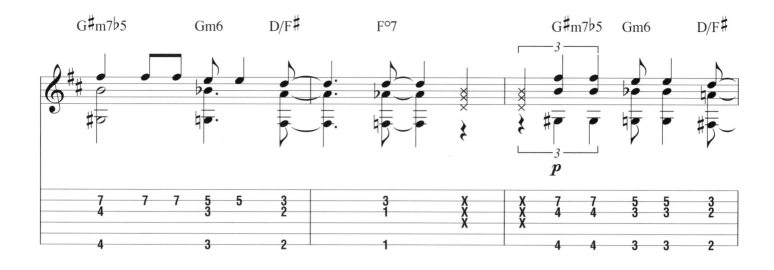

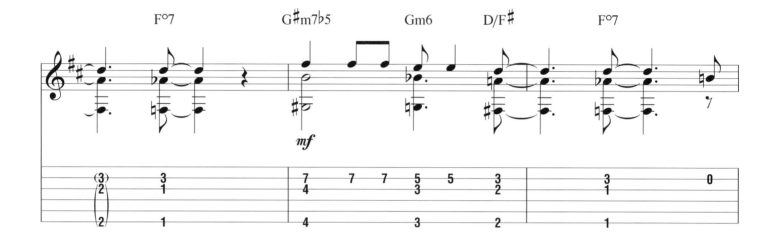

To Coda $\oplus$

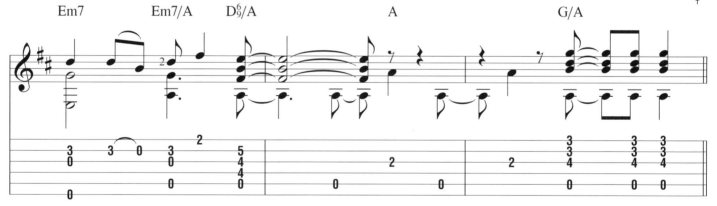

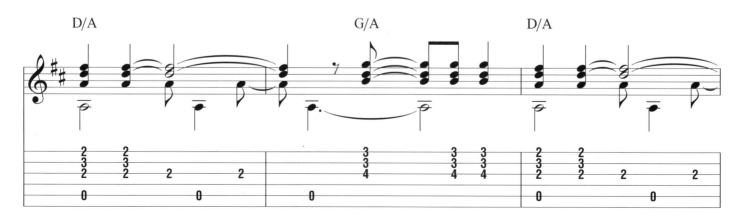

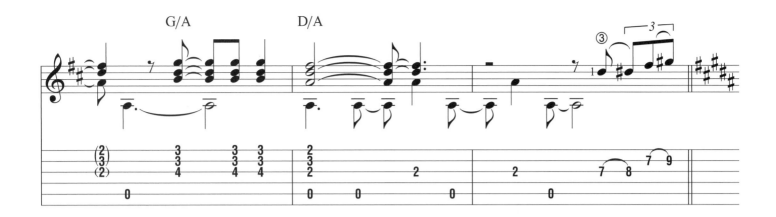

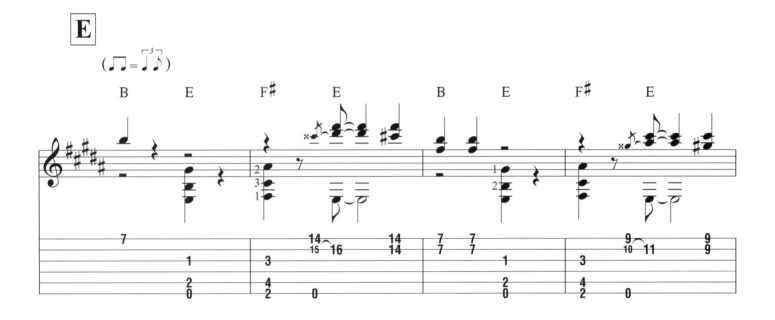

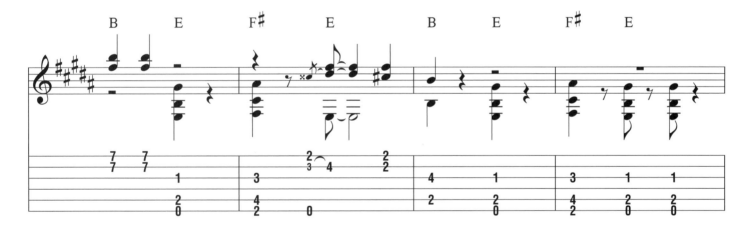

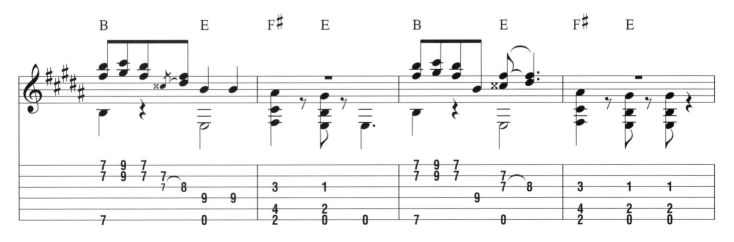

Coda

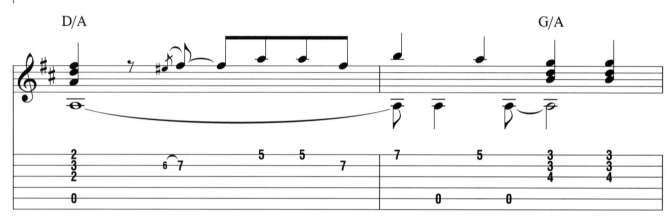

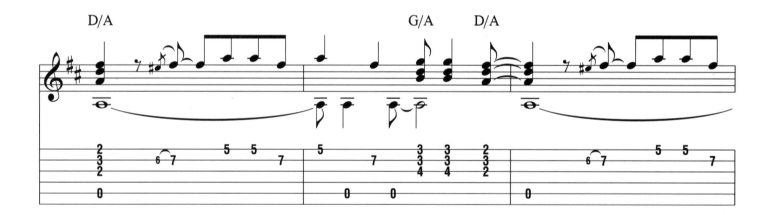

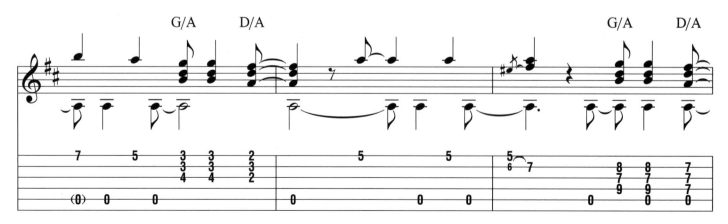

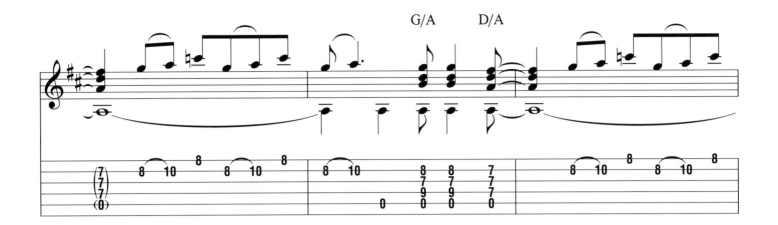

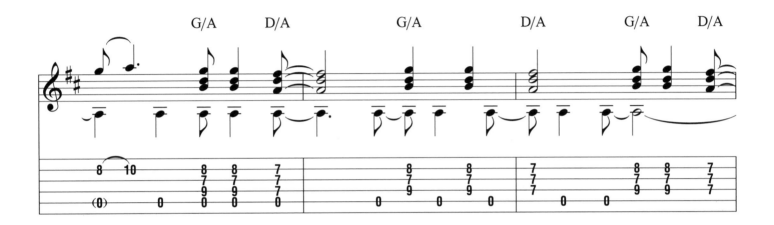

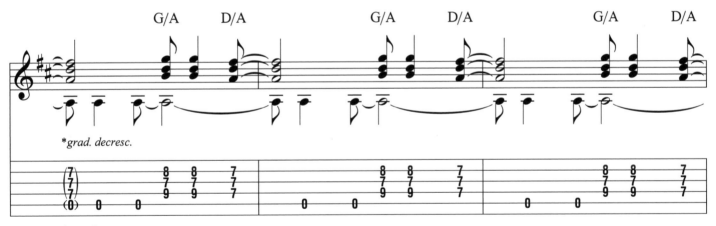

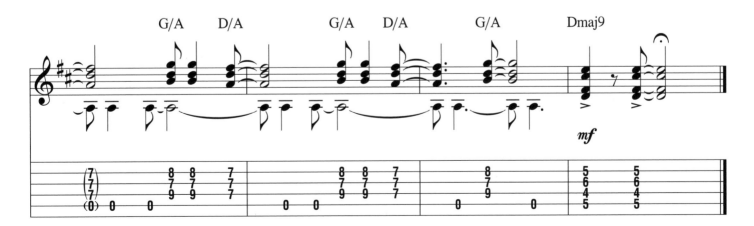

Für Elise

By Beethoven
Arranged by Vince Guaraldi

A

Moderately Fast ♩ = 130

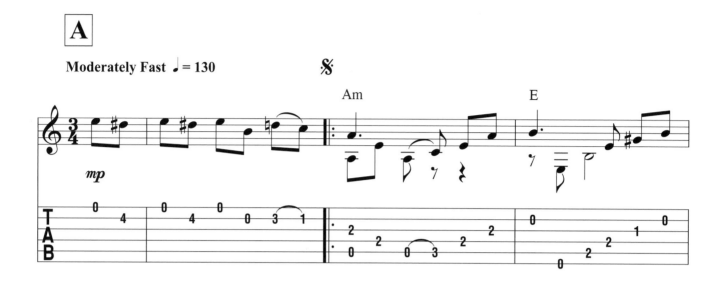

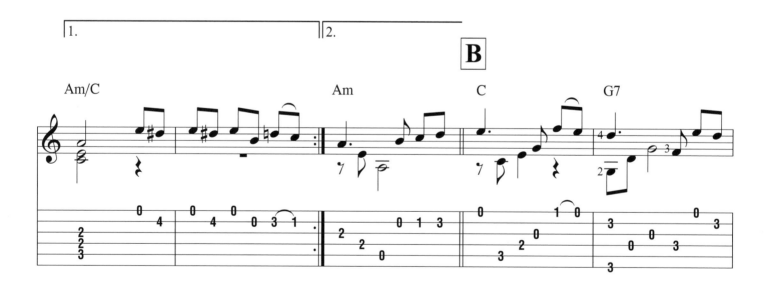

Copyright © 1965 LEE MENDELSON FILM PRODUCTIONS, INC.
Copyright Renewed
This arrangement Copyright © 2022 LEE MENDELSON FILM PRODUCTIONS, INC.
International Copyright Secured   All Rights Reserved

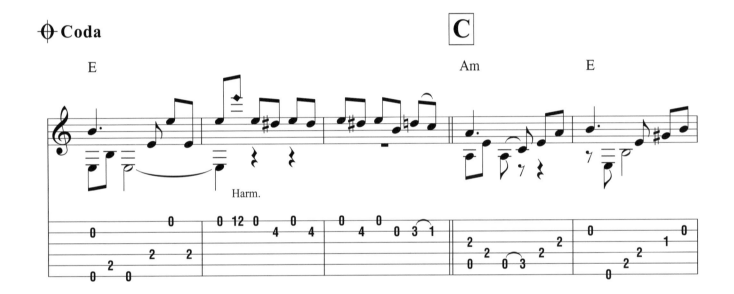

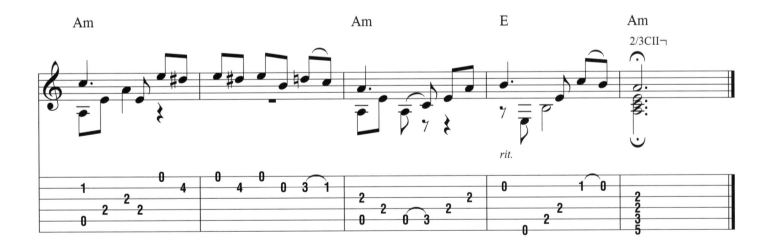

The Christmas Song
(Chestnuts Roasting on an Open Fire)
Music and Lyric by Mel Tormé and Robert Wells

Drop D tuning:
(low to high) D-A-D-G-B-E

Freely

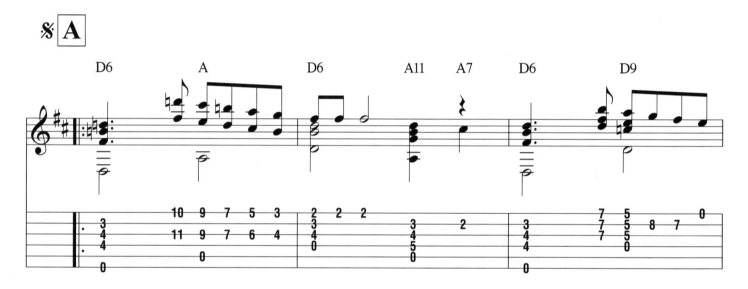

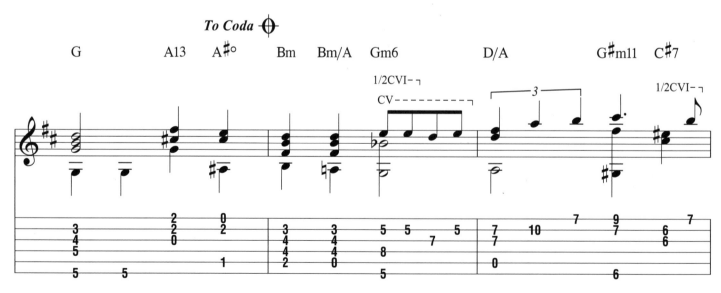

© 1946 (Renewed) EDWIN H. MORRIS & COMPANY, A Division of MPL Music Publishing, Inc. and SONY MUSIC PUBLISHING (US) LLC
This arrangement © 2022 EDWIN H. MORRIS & COMPANY, A Division of MPL Music Publishing, Inc. and SONY MUSIC PUBLISHING (US) LLC
All Rights on behalf of SONY MUSIC PUBLISHING (US) LLC Administered by
SONY MUSIC PUBLISHING (US) LLC, 424 Church Street, Suite 1200, Nashville, TN 37219
All Rights Reserved

PLAY THE CLASSICS

JAZZ FOLIOS FOR GUITARISTS

BEST OF JAZZ GUITAR
by Wolf Marshall • Signature Licks

In this book/audio pack, Wolf Marshall provides a hands-on analysis of 10 of the most frequently played tunes in the jazz genre, as played by the leading guitarists of all time. Features: All the Things You Are • How Insensitive • I'll Remember April • So What • Yesterdays • and more.
00695586 Book/Online Audio.............................. $29.99

GUITAR STANDARDS
Classic Jazz Masters Series

16 classic jazz guitar performances transcribed note for note with tablature: All of You (Kenny Burrell) • Easter Parade (Herb Ellis) • I'll Remember April (Grant Green) • Lover Man (Django Reinhardt) • Song for My Father (George Benson) • The Way You Look Tonight (Wes Montgomery) • and more. Includes a discography.
00699143 Guitar Transcriptions $14.95

JAZZ CLASSICS FOR SOLO GUITAR
arranged by Robert B. Yelin

This collection includes excellent chord melody arrangements in standard notation and tablature for 35 all-time jazz favorites: April in Paris • Cry Me a River • Day by Day • God Bless' the Child • It Might as Well Be Spring • Lover • My Romance • Nuages • Satin Doll • Tenderly • Unchained Melody • Wave • and more!
00699279 Solo Guitar $19.99

JAZZ FAVORITES FOR SOLO GUITAR
arranged by Robert B. Yelin

This fantastic 35-song collection includes lush chord melody arrangements in standard notation and tab: Autumn in New York • Call Me Irresponsible • How Deep Is the Ocean • I Could Write a Book • The Lady Is a Tramp • Mood Indigo • Polka Dots and Moonbeams • Solitude • Take the "A" Train • Where or When • more.
00699278 Solo Guitar $19.99

JAZZ GEMS FOR SOLO GUITAR
arranged by Robert B. Yelin

35 great solo arrangements of jazz classics, including: After You've Gone • Alice in Wonderland • The Christmas Song • Four • Meditation • Stompin' at the Savoy • Sweet and Lovely • Waltz for Debby • Yardbird Suite • You'll Never Walk Alone • You've Changed • and more.
00699617 Solo Guitar $19.99

JAZZ GUITAR BIBLE

The one book that has all of the jazz guitar classics transcribed note-for-note, with standard notation and tablature. Includes over 30 songs: Body and Soul • Girl Talk • I'll Remember April • In a Sentimental Mood • My Funny Valentine • Nuages • Satin Doll • So What • Stardust • Take Five • Tangerine • Yardbird Suite • and more.
00690466 Guitar Recorded Versions $27.99

JAZZ GUITAR CHORD MELODIES
arranged & performed by Dan Towey

This book/CD pack includes complete solo performances of 12 standards, including: All the Things You Are • Body and Soul • My Romance • How Insensitive • My One and Only Love • and more. The arrangements are performance level and range in difficulty from intermediate to advanced.
00698988 Book/CD Pack.. $19.95

JAZZ GUITAR PLAY-ALONG
Guitar Play-Along Volume 16

With this book/audio pack, all you have to do is follow the tab, listen to the online audio to hear how the guitar should sound, and then play along using the separate backing tracks. 8 songs: All Blues • Bluesette • Footprints • How Insensitive (Insensatez) • Misty • Satin Doll • Stella by Starlight • Tenor Madness.
00699584 Book/Online Audio.............................. $16.99

JAZZ STANDARDS FOR FINGERSTYLE GUITAR

20 songs, including: All the Things You Are • Autumn Leaves • Bluesette • Body and Soul • Fly Me to the Moon • The Girl from Ipanema • How Insensitive • I've Grown Accustomed to Her Face • My Funny Valentine • Satin Doll • Stompin' at the Savoy • and more.
00699029 Fingerstyle Guitar $17.99

JAZZ STANDARDS FOR SOLO GUITAR
arranged by Robert B. Yelin

35 chord melody guitar arrangements, including: Ain't Misbehavin' • Autumn Leaves • Bewitched • Cherokee • Darn That Dream • Girl Talk • I've Got You Under My Skin • Lullaby of Birdland • My Funny Valentine • A Nightingale Sang in Berkeley Square • Stella by Starlight • The Very Thought of You • and more.
00699277 Solo Guitar $19.99

101 MUST-KNOW JAZZ LICKS
by Wolf Marshall

Add a jazz feel and flavor to your playing! 101 definitive licks, plus demonstration audio, from every major jazz guitar style, neatly organized into easy-to-use categories. They're all here: swing and pre-bop, bebop, post-bop modern jazz, hard bop and cool jazz, modal jazz, soul jazz and postmodern jazz.
00695433 Book/Online Audio.............................. $19.99

Visit Hal Leonard Online at **www.halleonard.com**

Prices, contents and availability subject to change without notice.